Just Jesus.

by Marjie Schaefer

www.FlourishThroughTheWord.com

© 2015 by Marjie Schaefer. All rights reserved. No part of this document may be reproduced or transmitted in any form by any means, electronic, mechanical, photocopying, recording, or otherwise, without prior written permission of Marjie Schaefer.

Dedication

This study came about from the request of friends who desired a short-term Bible study for the summer. I had never written a study that would take participants through an entire book of the Bible, and the task was daunting. The year before, I had attended a *Just Give Me Jesus* Conference hosted by Anne Graham Lotz. While there, I was taught a Bible study method that enabled me to study the book of Ephesians and create what you now hold in your hands.

I am so grateful for the many eternal investments that have been deposited into me. This first study is lovingly dedicated to my mother, Linda Lovett. My mom is the one who modeled for me how to be in the Word of God on a daily basis. I would not be who I am today without her influence and instruction.

A note from Marjie before you begin....

The Message Bible says it this way: "***It's in Christ that we find out who we are and what we are living for.***" (Ephesians 1:11)

This sums up the book of Ephesians in a nutshell: it really is all about Jesus and His finished work on the cross—***Just Jesus***. Nothing more needs to be added to what He has done and secured for us.

Called the 'Grand Canyon of Scripture' due to its depth and breadth, Ephesians is also profoundly practical for our daily lives.

This study will equip you in many ways if you set aside the time each day to complete the homework.

The daily studies are designed to take you deeper into the Word for yourself. There are Greek words and definitions to help expand your understanding of the language used by Paul as he wrote to this ancient church.

The same Bible study method I used to write the study is a part of this study with the intention of developing your personal investigation of the Word.

Someone has said: ***The Bible is the only book in the world that when you read it, the Author shows up!***

Also included in this study is a *Special Equipping Section*, where you are encouraged to record your discoveries of the majesty of Jesus, your identity in Christ, and your expressions of gratitude.

You are also encouraged to say these things out loud because faith comes by hearing, and hearing by the Word of God. Whenever you see the megaphone in these pages, you are encouraged to take a few minutes and vocalize the truths of God's Word.

Paul had an incredibly deep prayer life and there is much for us to learn from him in this area. He wrote in Ephesians 1:17: *"I keep asking that....you may know him better."* Paul knew that prayer was a way to get more of God Himself, that prayer really is taking hold of God.

In this study, we will examine the prayers of Paul so that we can get a hold of God for ourselves and deepen our personal prayer lives.

There is so much treasure to be found in this 'Grand Canyon of Scripture'. Are you ready to go to the depths and explore what God has to say to you through His Word?

Albert Einstein said, "I want to know God's thoughts. All the rest are just details." This study is designed and written with the prayerful intention that we will know God's thoughts as we dig deeper into His Word.

Let's go together and see more of Him!

Marjie

Ephesians... a little background

The city of Ephesus was once the greatest Roman city in Asia Minor, with a population of 250,000. According to Greek legend, the city had been founded by the Amazons, mythical female warriors.

The Greeks had lived there for a thousand years and had been conquered by Alexander the Great. The Romans acquired the city in 133 B.C and made it the capital of Asia.

Ephesus was the main line of communication between Rome and the East. Merchants and traders flocked to it. Pilgrims came from all over Asia Minor to Ephesus to worship. This was because the city was devoted to the cult worship of the Greek goddess, Artemis, which became identified with the Roman goddess, Diana.

The marble temple to Diana stretched longer than our modern-day football fields. The columns on the temple rose sixty feet high. Here also stood the masterpieces of the famous sculptors of Greece. The temple was considered one of the Seven Wonders of the World.

The temple was built upon a marsh, and today, the water has reclaimed it. Only a few columns exist today.

Paul preached faith in Christ in Ephesus with tremendous impact. Local artists had grown rich selling amulets and images of Diana to her many followers. As people became Christians, they would no longer buy these pagan charms and tokens.

As converts to Christianity grew, sales declined and the artists were not happy with Paul and sought to rid the city of him.

We have three Biblical windows into the city of Ephesus: Acts, Revelation, and the Letter to the Ephesians. The Book of Revelation tells the story of the church that became so engrossed in religion, it lost sight of a relationship with Jesus. The church in Ephesus was warned that Christ would come and remove their lampstand.

Today, there is no city or church in the location that was once Ephesus. Today in Izmir, Turkey, Islam is the predominant religion in that area that was once thoroughly evangelized by Paul.

The treasure we do have today is Paul's letter to the church in Ephesus. His letter is all about our awesome blessings of grace and our spiritual authority in Christ.

The letter falls into two parts: belief and behavior—or doctrinal: the facts of our redemption, and practical: how we are to live.

In The Message Bible's introduction to Ephesians, Eugene Peterson says it this way: *"What we know about God and what we do for God have a way of getting broken apart in our lives. The moment the organic unity of belief and behavior is damaged in any way, we are incapable of living out the full humanity for which we were created.*

Paul's letter to the Ephesians joins together what has been torn apart in our sin-wrecked world. He begins with an exuberant exploration of what Christians believe about God, and then, like a surgeon skillfully setting a compound fracture, 'sets' this belief in God into our behavior before God so that the bones—belief and behavior—knit together and heal."

This book abounds with spiritual riches, yet it is intensely practical for our daily lives.

WEEK ONE

Day One

The Prayer Life of Paul

Grace-Charis (Khar'-ece)-Strong's #5485-Divine favor and blessing; that which affords joy, pleasure, delight, sweetness, charm, loveliness: grace of speech; good will; loving-kindness; the divine influence upon the heart and its reflection in the life; reflecting gratitude.

Ephesians 1: 1-14

1. Read the first fourteen verses out of several translations. We are told in verse 3 that we have been blessed with *'every spiritual blessing in the heavenly places in Christ."* List these out here:

    - _____ (v. 4)

    - _____ (v. 4)

    - _____ (v. 4)

    - _____ (v. 4)

    - _____ (v. 5)

    - _____ (v. 5)

    - _____ (v. 6)

    - _____ (v. 6)

- _____ (v. 7)

- _____ (v. 7)

- _____ (v. 8)

- _____ (v. 9)

- _____ (v. 11)

- _____ (v. 11)

- _____ (v. 13)

- _____ (v. 13-14)

2. Spend some time today giving thanks for each one of these blessings. Choose 2-3 that are especially meaningful to you at this season in your life, and put them on index cards. Keep the cards with you each day this week, thanking God for these blessings and praising Him for loving you so well.

Day Two

Read **Ephesians 1:15-23**
(out of several different translations if you are able.)

1. What 2 outstanding qualities were the Ephesians known for?
   _____ and _____ (v. 15)

2. According to v. 16, what did Paul never stop doing and why do you think this is important?

3. List out the specifics Paul requests of God in his prayer for the Ephesians:
   - _____ (v. 17)

   - _____ (v. 18)

   - _____ (v. 18)

   - _____ (v. 18)

   - _____ (v. 19)

4. According to verse 21, where is Jesus now seated?

5. What are the 5 things Jesus is 'far above' according to v. 21?

6. Look up the following verses and write the phrases that confirm Paul's statement in Ephesians 1: 20-21.

   Psalm 110:1

   Isaiah 9:6-7

   Luke 1:32

   Philippians 2:9-10

   Psalm 8:6

Day Three

Re-read Ephesians 1:16-19

 Spend time today reading these verses **_out loud_** in different translations.

1. After doing this, re-work the specific prayer of Paul, personalizing it for yourself in the space below.

2. In verses 19-23, we are encouraged by the facts of the working power of Christ in our lives. Summarize what you learn from these verses and tell how these truths impact your daily life.

3. In verse 23, the body of Christ is mentioned. What is the physical presence of Christ today? What is this current presence to be filled with?

- Go to the "*Special Equipping Section*" of your workbook and write out what you have gleaned from your study of chapter one. List your findings in the Majesty of Jesus and My Daily Declarations.

   Make sure you say these **out loud** before you end for the day!

Day Four

Our Journey Through Chapter Two Begins!
Read Ephesians 2:1-10

1. Fill in the chart below based on v. 1-10 and be sure to list the verses beside each statement.

   Who I Was Before Christ: **Who I am In Christ:**

2. In verse 2, who is Paul referencing as the 'prince of the power of the air'? To better answer this question, turn to John 12:31 and Ephesians 6:11-12. Why do you think we need to take note of this 'prince'?

3. Who is another 'Prince' that Scripture mentions in Isaiah 9:6?

4. Who is this 'Prince of Peace' and what does He offer us according to Ephesians 2:14, John 14:27, and Isaiah 26:3?

5. In verses 5 and 8, we see that we are saved by _____.

Day Five

 Pray the personalized prayer **out loud** from Day 2 and give God thanks for the spiritual blessings in your life.

Read Ephesians 2: 11-18

- What title or heading would you give this section of the Epistle?

Some background......_The term 'uncircumcision' is the most direct way to describe the fact that Gentiles, or anyone who was not a Jew, were outside any covenant relationship with God. Before Jesus made available to us the "New Covenant" through His sacrificial death on the cross, Gentiles were excluded from citizenship in Israel, and could not partake of the covenant promises of God. For a Gentile, there was no hope and no ability to know God's presence in the world. Christ's death enabled Gentiles who were far from God to be grafted in to enjoy and partake of God's covenant promises_

1. Using Ephesians 2:11-18 list the verse beside each statement.

   Outside the Covenant   **Inside the Covenant**

2. According to Ephesians 2:13-14, what is the one way that you have been brought into covenant relationship with God?

Read Ephesians 2:19-22

3. In v. 19, what are the Gentiles referred to?

4. What is Jesus named in verse 20? (Be sure and list this in your "Special Section")

5. What image is expressed in verses 20-22? What do you think it means to be a 'dwelling place of God in the Spirit' (v. 22)?

WEEK TWO

Day One

Ephesians 3-The Mystery
Read Ephesians 3:1-7

1. For what reason is Paul a prisoner? (clue: review Eph. 2:22)

2. What is the 'mystery' Paul is writing about?

Greek Word:
Mystery-Musterion (moos-tay-ree-on)-Strong's #3466-a secret known; something hidden that requires special revelation. In the New Testament, the word denotes something that people could never know by their own understanding. It requires revelation from God. The secret thoughts, plans and dispensations of God remain hidden from unsaved mankind, but are rather revealed to all believers.

3. In verse 4, Paul uses the phrase "when you read." What is he assuming that believers are doing? Why is this important?

4. What 2 things in this passage do you see that the Holy Spirit does for believers?

5. Go to your "*Special Equipping Section*" and fill in the appropriate pages with what you have seen from your study today and make your "Daily Declarations!"

Days Two and Three

A Bible Study Method

Today you will learn (by doing) a Bible study method that will greatly enhance your own personal understanding of the Scriptures. This is the exact method I used while preparing for this Bible study.

I used this to do a verse-by-verse analysis of the book of Ephesians. I was first introduced to this study when I attended a "Just Give Me Jesus" conference in Seattle, taught by Anne Graham Lotz.

You will have 2 days to work on this method so that you have ample time to work through each verse.

I have done the first verse for you so that you get an idea of how to work it. Take your time and ask the Holy Spirit to be your teacher. We will be using this method one time each week throughout the rest of our homework, so don't get discouraged if you don't get the hang of it this first time. Enjoy!

*Read Ephesians 3:8-13

Step 1-List the facts verse by verse. What does the verse say?

Step 2-What spiritual lessons do you learn from the facts? What does it mean?

Step 3-Application-What does it mean for you personally?

<u>**Step one:**</u> Verse 8: Paul, the least of the saints, has grace given to preach the riches of Christ to the Gentiles.

<u>**Step two:**</u> Paul understood his humble position as he proclaimed the loftiest message.

<u>**Step three:**</u> Do I walk in humility as I proclaim truth to others?

Now finish verses 9-13 on your own, using this method.

 Go to your *"Special Equipping Section"* and fill in the appropriate pages with any new discoveries you have made from your 2-day study using this method. Be sure and make your declarations **out loud**!

Days Four and Five

Another Grand Prayer From Paul
Ephesians 3:14-21

1. In verse 16, what does Paul specifically ask God to do?

2. What is the message of Philippians 4:13?

3. Read another prayer of Paul in Colossians 1:9-11. What is he asking God to do here?

Greek Word:
Strengthened-Dunamoo (Doo-nam-ah-oh)-Strong's #1412-To make strong; confirm; enable. Here is the family of Duna-power words:

Dunami- to be able

Danamis—power; usually supernatural

Dunastes—sovereign or ruler

Dunateo—to be mighty

Dunatos--powerful

4. How do these Scriptures and the understanding of the Greek word for strengthened, make a difference in the way you will pray this for yourself and for others?

5. Paul prayed in v. 17 that Christ would dwell in our hearts through faith. How do John 14:23 and Romans 8:9 fit with Paul's request?

For greater understanding.... *"Spirit" or pneuma in the Greek, means breath, breeze, or current of air. Pneuma—or our spirit— is that part of a person capable of responding to God.*

The Holy Spirit is the third Person of salvation, empowers us to live the victorious life, and to understand the Bible, to pray and to evangelize.

6. In v. 18, Paul prays that we may 'be able to comprehend'…. How is this similar to what he prayed in Ephesians 1:18 and what does this mean for us?

7. What are the 2 things asked for in v. 19?
   Compare this request with the request in Ephesians 1:23. What do you think this means for you personally?

Verse 20 is an amazing statement about God! For greater clarity:

Greek word:
Abundantly-Perissos (Per-is-sos)-Strong's
#4053- Superabundance; excessive; overflowing surplus; over and above; more than enough; profuse; extraordinary; more than sufficient.

Ask-Aiteo (ahee-the-oh)-Strong's #154-To request; petition. This word denotes insistent asking (not demanding) without qualms, presenting a request, knowing He longs to answer and give.

8. From your 2-day study of this prayer, re-write it and personalize it in such a way that you are able to aiteo-ask-petition God for yourself in the space below. It may be helpful to 'bullet point' the specifics.

9. Now combine this prayer that you just wrote out along with your earlier prayer (Week 1 Homework) on the following page. This will now be the prayer you use going forward when you are directed to pray aloud the Ephesians prayers.

The Ephesians 1 & 3 Prayers:

WEEK THREE

Day One

Practical, purposeful, powerful living through unity
Ephesians 4

Read Ephesians 4:1-6—Walking in Unity: "*And mark that you do this with humility and discipline...but steadily pouring yourselves out for each other in acts of love, alert at noticing differences and quick at mending fences.* **Everything you are and think and do is permeated with oneness**.*" (Ephesians 4:3 & 6-The Message Bible)*

Bible Study Method—Use this method again on verses 1-6:

Step 1-List the facts verse by verse.

Step 2-What spiritual lessons do you learn from the facts?

Step 3-What is the personal application for you?

1. Based on your own investigation, what are some actions to be avoided that would disrupt unity in the church?

2. Why is unity among believers (the church) so important?

Days Two and Three

Spiritual Gifts
Ephesians 4:7-16

1. Read the passage for today. In verse 7, what was given to each one of us?

Greek Word:
Gift-Charisma-(khar-is-mah); Strong's #5486; Related to other words derived from char---chara isis gift of grace, a free gift, divine gratuity, spiritual endowment.

Read **1 Corinthians 12:4-11** to answer the following questions:

2. Why are the gifts of the Spirit given?

3. Who gives these gifts?

4. What is the 'common denominator' regarding the gifts in this passage?

5. What is the purpose of the gifts according to Ephesians 4:12?

6. What is the ultimate two-pronged purpose of the gifts in Ephesians 4:13?

Greek Word:
Equipping-Katartismos-(kat-ar-tis-moss)-Strong's #2677-Making fit, preparing, training, perfecting, making fully qualified for service. In classical language, the word means setting a bone during surgery. The Great Physician is making all necessary adjustments so the Church will not be 'out of joint'.

7. Is the work of ministry in the 'body of Christ' (the church) just for a select few leaders? Why or why not?

8. In v. 14-15 of Ephesians 4, we see 4 benefits of being equipped. What are they?

- v.14

- v.14

- v.15

- v.15

9. Verse 16 is a similar message to what Paul had to say in Ephesians 2:19-22. Re-read those verses in chapter 2 with verse 16 and summarize the central point Paul was making to the church.

10. Take a spiritual gifts test on-line today. Go to SpiritualGiftsTest.com for a free version available to you.

Be prepared to share your results with your group at our next gathering.

Day Four

A Lifestyle Fashioned By God
Ephesians 4:17-24

Paul, in this section, now turns his attention to more individualized lifestyle aspects of being equipped. Earlier, he spoke to the church: "Use your gifts to build up and make the 'body of Christ' as effective, fruitful and unified as possible." Now, Paul targets the individual in the way she should 'walk' and talk.

Read these 7 verses several times to get the gist of what Paul is saying. (Remember: "Gentiles" are considered to be unsaved; the non-believers.)

1. In v. 17-19, list the 5 traits of a worldly walk:

2. Summarize these traits in one word: _____

3. Contrast the 'old man' with the 'new man' in v. 20-24:

    OLD   **NEW**

4. The believer ('new man') has a newly created capacity for a lifestyle of obedience. How is this possible based on Ephesians 2:10 and Ephesians 3:16?

5. Paul gives 3 specific commands to all believers in v. 22-24, what are they?

- v. 22

- v. 23

- v. 24

If these are commands given to us in Scripture, then the Lord intends for us to *obey* them! They are not suggestions or options, but rather, specific things we are to do. How are we able and equipped to obey these commands?

Day Five

Do Not Grieve the Holy Spirit
Ephesians 4:25-32

We have seen from our study yesterday that as believers there are things we must do and must not do. However, we are not to take this action on our own. We have an internal power source: The Holy Spirit—our Helper, Counselor, Comforter and Guide. The Precious Holy Spirit—Jesus living inside of us. We can grieve (to distress; cause injury to; offend; vex; sadden) Him by our sinful actions and attitudes. This is seen very clearly and dramatically in this portion of Paul's letter.

Read Ephesians 4:25-32

1. Again, we read the command to 'put off' or put away certain conduct and to do the opposite. List the verse reference beside each action step below.

    Conduct To Put Off   Positive Action To Take

2. In v. 26, Paul gives the 'freedom' to be _____. This is not an invitation to be angry! He knows that as emotional humans, we will encounter things and people that will anger us. Jesus said in the Gospels that "offenses **will** come"—but how we respond to these offenses will have a tremendous impact on our emotional and spiritual health.

   Paul is actually quoting a psalm here! Read Psalm 4:4-5: What is the antidote given here for dealing with anger?

   _____

3. In Psalm 37:8, what does anger cause? _____

4. Ephesians 4:27 is an aspect of the 'harm' anger can cause. Have you ever thought of your anger 'giving place' to the devil? What do you think that means?

5. The power of our mouths: **"Watch the way you talk. Let nothing foul or dirty come out of your mouth. Say only what helps, each word a gift." (Eph. 4:29-The Message Biblc).**

"Let no foul or polluting language, nor evil word nor unwholesome or worthless talk (ever) come out of your mouth, but only such (speech) as is good and beneficial to the spiritual progress of others, as is fitting to the need and the occasion, that it may be a blessing and give grace (God's favor) to those who hear it. (Eph. 4: 29-The Amplified Bible).

- In Col. 3:8-10, where do we see most of these things to be 'put off' originating?

- Ex. 4:11-Who made your mouth?

- Psalm 37:30-What does a righteous mouth speak?

- Proverbs 13:3-What 2 things can happen with our mouths?

- Matthew 15:11-What defiles a person?

- Matthew 12:34-What is revealed by what comes out of our mouths?

- Romans 10:10-What is made with our mouths?

- In light of your study of these verses, what conclusions can you summarize about the use of our words?

State the importance of why we are speaking our faith **out loud** (our "Daily Declarations") in this 6-week journey?

"The way we talk matters. We need to think deeply about the theological implications of what we are saying and remember that God is not simply a useful tool to support...our beliefs. God is the Powerful Center. For our soul and the soul of others, it is worth thinking before we speak. Talk matters. The way we speak and what we say paint a picture of God in our hearts and minds. Not only do our words reflect our theology, they can also shape our theology. And what we say and the way we say it enters the ear and fires the neurons and deposits our concepts of God into our brains. Theology is not simply thoughts or ideas about God---it is what emerges from our lips as a result of those things. The way we talk about God has been shaped by our view of Him---and observing the way we talk about God can help us to check our theology."

~From the book, <u>Looking For God</u>, by Nancy Ortberg, 2008, Tyndale House Publishing.

"Let all bitterness and indignation and wrath (passion, rage, bad temper) and resentment (anger, animosity) and quarreling (brawling, clamor, contention) and slander (evil-speaking, abusive or blasphemous language) be banished from you, with all malice (spite, ill will, or baseness of any kind). And become useful and helpful and kind to one another, tenderhearted (compassionate, understanding, loving-hearted), forgiving one another (readily and freely), as God in Christ forgave you." (Ephesians 4:31-32-the Amplified Bible)

6. **Forgiveness** is the 'hallmark' of our Christian experience, life and character. Our own relationship with Jesus begins with His forgiveness secured for us on the cross. He then expects no less from us---forgiving others as He forgave us.

   a. Read 2 examples of the teaching of Jesus on forgiveness in Matthew 6:14-15 and Matthew 18:21-35, then answer the following questions:

b. What is the basis of our forgiving others?

c. What is fundamental to having our prayers of forgiveness answered?

d. What else do you learn about forgiveness from these verses?

e. Is there anyone the Holy Spirit is bringing to mind that you need to forgive?

Prayerfully review the last 2 days of your study before coming to Bible study. Go to your "*Special Equipping Section*" and fill in the appropriate pages.

 Conclude your devotional time with your "Daily Declarations"!

WEEK FOUR

Day One

Walking in Love
Ephesians 5

Ephesians 5:1-7
- Do the Bible study method on these seven verses.

Step 1-What does the passage say? Be literal.

Step 2-What does it mean? Be spiritual.

Step 3-What does it mean to you personally? Be practical.

v.1

v.2

v.3

v.4

v.5

v.6

v.7

- What has the Holy Spirit specifically said to you from this passage?

- Go to the *"Special Equipping Section"* and:
  1) List any Name or reference to Christ you have found.

  2) List any "Identity Markers" you have found and list them in your "Daily Declarations".

  3) Speak all of these ***out loud!***

Day Two

Walking In the Light
Ephesians 5:8-14

   Pray **out loud** the prayers listed from Chapters 1 & 3.

1. Paul is doing another notable contrast here (read the verses listed!). What metaphor does he use this time?
   _____and _____ (v. 8)

2. As being 'light in the Lord', write out the specific directions that reflect our heavenly light:

   - v. 8
   - v. 10
   - v. 11
   - v. 12
   - v. 14

3. In verse 9, Paul assumes his readers know what the fruit of the Spirit is. He says this 'fruit' <u>is in</u> all goodness, righteousness and truth. Read Galatians 5:22 and list out the specific "fruit".

Greek Word:
Goodness- Agathosune- (ag-ath-oh-soo-nay)-Strong's #19- Beneficence; kindness in actual manifestations; virtue equipped for action; a bountiful propensity both to will and to do what is good.

4. How do we find out what is acceptable to the Lord as stated in v. 10?

5. You've already visited this Scripture, but write down the specific things that reveal what is acceptable to God from Romans 12:1-2.

6. In Ephesians 5:12, another reference is made to speaking. Why do you think Paul gave this warning?

Day Three

Walking in Wisdom
Ephesians 5:15-21

Wisdom is something we all long for. The Bible teaches us over and over again to simply ask for it. Paul makes the request for wisdom an integral part of his prayers for the Ephesians ('asking God to give you the spirit of wisdom..."). Hopefully, you have been making this request an integral part of your prayers as well.

Let's take some time to do that before we begin this brief study on wisdom. Turn to the "prayer" section of your workbook and spend some time asking God for the 'spirit of wisdom and revelation'.

1. Paul appears to *love* contrasts! Here he gives us another one in v. 15: _____ vs. _____.

2. What does it mean to 'redeem the time' and to 'walk circumspectly'? (See Colossians 4:5 for a similar command from Paul.)

3. List out all the specific directives from Paul in v. 15-21:

4. What would you entitle this list?

5. In verse 18, the command is given to not be drunk with wine. What is the context of this command?

6. What further insight does Proverbs 20:1 add to our context?

7. What does verse 18 direct the believer to do?

8. Is there direction given with how to 'be filled'? What contributes to a spiritual walk? (see verses 18-21)

We've been taught that there is one Spirit and that He has given us gifts (grace) and He is our internal Power Source. He enables us to walk in wisdom and to live our lives in a God-fashioned lifestyle, influencing and transforming all aspects of our lives.

Days Four and Five

Christ and the Church—aka—Marriage!
Ephesians 5:22-33

God desires our lives to reflect the fullness of the Holy Spirit, where our relationships—both familial and vocational—are transformed and are built on the foundation of mutual respect (see Ephesians 5:21).

1. In verse 22, what is the command given to wives?

    Submit-Hupotasso-(hoop-ot-as-so)-Strong's #5293-to be under; obedience; to make subject to; to submit self to; literally to stand under.

2. In what attitude or mindset is a woman to submit to her husband?

    What is *your* attitude towards the Lord?

    How is a husband to relate to his wife?

3. We've looked at how Christ provides all things (every spiritual blessing in the heavenlies) for His body (the church). Do a quick review of all the things we receive from Christ through His finished work on the cross in Ephesians 1(the spiritual blessings). Who do you think has a tougher job, husbands or wives—in light of the Biblical requirements?

4. Read these 2 Scriptures and tell how Christ loves the church-- Acts 20:28 & Ephesians 5:25:

5. Verses 24-25 give the thrust of Paul's message in this section of the letter, and he lays out the 3 strands of relationship. Beside each one, write the Biblical standards for each:
    a. **Church to Christ:**

    b. **Wives to Husbands:**

    c. **Husbands to Wives:**

6. In verses 26-27 & 29, list the other things Christ did/does for the church:

7. In verse 31, Paul quotes an Old Testament passage. Turn there now and read it in Genesis 2:23-24. Jesus also quoted it in Matthew 19:3-8. How do these help you to understand the Ephesians passage?

8. What is the relationship between 'cleaving' and 'submission'?

9. Jesus warned that hardness of heart in a marriage would be dangerous to the relationship. What else does Scripture link hardness of heart to according to the following verses:

- Mark 16:14-
- Matthew 5:32-
- Daniel 5:20-

10. In verses 30 & 32, Paul reminds us that the marriage relationship is really a picture of Christ and the church. Do you regularly consider that you are the flesh and bones of Jesus on the earth today?

Summarize what you have learned about Christ today and list it in your *"Special Equipping Section"*.

Take some time to declare these truths out loud.

WEEK FIVE

Day One

The Family in the Lord

1. Read Ephesians 6:1-4 and do the Bible study method based on these four verses:

   Step 1-List the facts.

   Step 2-List the spiritual lessons.

   Step 3-List the applications.

   Obey-Hupakouo-(hoop-ak-oo-oh)-Strong's #5219-To hear as a subordinate; listen attentively; obey as a subject; answer and respond; submit without reservation. The word contains the ideas of hearing, responding, and obeying.

2. Look up the related Scriptures and record your insights or any additional information given.

   - Colossians 3:20

   - Deuteronomy 5:16

   - Genesis 18:19

*"If it was going to be easy to raise kids,
it never would have started ~Anonymous~*

"In what we stress with our children, how do I know if I'm keeping first things first? Ask your children a very insightful question: 'What do you think your dad and mom feel the most passionate about?' Does the Gospel come to mind as they answer? Our kids probably best reveal whether or not our hearts are mirroring what God desires us to be."

~Gary Thomas, Sacred Parenting~

Day Two

Godly Living in the Marketplace
Ephesians 6:5-9

1. What is the believer's calling and duty in the marketplace according to this passage?

2. The following Scriptures reveal truths and principles not just for the marketplace, but for life! Look up each passage and record the life-giving principles that apply to all:

    - Colossians 3:22-24

    - 1 Timothy 6:1-2

    - Titus 2:9-10

    - 1 Peter 2:18-22

    - Ecclesiastes 9:10

3. Ephesians 6:9 declares an amazing truth about our "Master in heaven". Pray over this truth and ask the Holy Spirit to 'seal it' in your heart and mind. Is there anything in your life that needs adjusting?

Partiality-Prosopolepsia-(Pros-oh-pol-ape-see-ah)-
Strong's #4382- favoritism; partiality; distinction; bias, conditional preference. The word denotes a biased judgment, which gives respect to rank, position or circumstances instead of considering the intrinsic conditions. God shows no partiality in justice, judgment or favorable treatment when dealing with people and He expects us to follow His example.

> Go to your *Special Equipping Section:* Record on the "Majesty of Christ" page and your "Daily Declarations" page.

 Spend some time today going through each page and saying these **out loud**!

Why Do We Need Armor Anyway?

Spiritual warfare is real, whether it is acknowledged or ignored. Military language and warfare fills the pages of the Bible. The sounds of warfare echo from Genesis to Revelation. Throughout the Scriptures, weapons play a major role. Weapons in the Bible many times refer to literal tools of warfare, whether defensive like a shield or offensive like a sword. But even in many of these contexts, we observe that weapons stand for more than a struggle for political and military power—they are the tools in the battle of God against the forces of evil.

In the New Testament, a definite transition occurs from physical warfare to spiritual warfare. When the mob arrived to arrest Jesus, the Gospels report that Peter used his sword to strike the servant of the high priest, cutting off his ear. Jesus responds by saying: "Put your sword back in its place...for all who draw the sword will die by the sword. Do you think I cannot call on my Father and He will at once put at my disposal more than twelve legions of angels?" (Matthew 26:52-53 NIV). **Jesus then goes to the cross where He defeats Satan, not by killing him---but by dying.**

*The following is an excerpt from John Eldredge's book, <u>Epic—The Story God Is Telling</u>:

"Why does every story have a villain?

It's hard to think of a tale without one. As children, we learned to fear the Big Bad Wolf and the Troll under the bridge. As we grew older, we discovered more serious villains in the Star Wars series—Darth Vader and Darth Maul and Darth Sidious. The Wicked Witch of the West hunted Dorothy. Wallace fought against Longshanks, and Maximus went hand to hand against Commodus. In The Fellowship of the Ring, we come to dread the Dark Lord Sauron, the Orcs that do his bidding, and the Black Riders who hunt poor Frodo and the ring that will give the evil one power to enslave the world.

Every story has a villain because yours does.

Most people do not live as though the Story has a Villain, and that makes life very confusing. How have we missed this? All the stories we've been telling about the presence of evil power in the world, all the dark characters that have sent chills down our spines and given us restless nights---they are spoken to us as warnings.

There is evil cast around us.

War. Famine. Betrayal. Murder. Surely we know there is an evil force in this world. Where did it come from? What is its motive? How are we to find refuge from its claws?

You can learn something about a story by the characters the author writes into it. Knights and a dragon are going to give you a certain kind of tale---a tale that chipmunks and acorns cannot provide. The presence of the Jedi warriors ennobles and endangers those dramas, just as we know something serious is about to unfold when we send the marines or the Special Forces to the coast of some distant land.

What does it mean when God sets the stage with the universe's equivalent of the Navy Seals or the Delta Force? They are powerful, they are armed, and they are dangerous.

Perhaps this Story is not nearly as 'safe' as we'd like to believe.

This is precisely what the Bible (and all the stories that echo it) has warned us about all these years: we live in two worlds—or in one world with two halves, part that we can see and part that we cannot. We are urged, for our own welfare, to act as though the unseen world (the rest of reality) is, in fact, more weighty and more real and more dangerous than the part of reality we can see."

This is why we need the "Armor of God": to effectively stand against the spiritual forces of wickedness that bombard God's people on a daily basis. I thought John Eldredge's narrative about the Great Story was well put, which is why I included a portion of it here for you to read before you delve into your own personal study of the spiritual armor. It paints a poignant picture of the reality of the unseen world.

May God bless your study.

Day Three

The Whole Armor of God--
Being Strong in the Lord's Power!
Ephesians 6:10-20

1. In verse 10, the command is given to _____ _____ in the Lord and in His power.

2. Paul now gives practical instruction on how to be strong in God's power. In verse 11, what are we instructed to do?

3. The word 'wiles' is translated 'methodia' from the Greek in which we get our word method or strategy. Who is our enemy and what does he do? Use the following to answer:
- Revelation 12:9-10
- John 8:44
- Matthew 4:3
- 1 John 5:19
- John 10:10
- 1 Peter 5:8-9

4. Why does he act with such urgency according to Revelation 12:12?

5. What are we *not* wrestling against according to Ephesians 6:12?

6. List out the 4-pronged hierarchy that we are wrestling against (v. 12):
   -
   -
   -
   -

7. List the 2 things we are to do as believers engaged in this invisible warfare:

   Are we instructed to fight?

The Spiritual War

- Stronghold-anything opposing God's will; first established in the mind by wrong thinking. Remember: our enemy is a deceiver, accuser and father of lies---this is why we are to take every thought captive and make it obey Christ.
- At the base (root) of every stronghold is a **lie**---a place of bondage where God's Word has been compromised, maligned, disregarded, or ignored.
- At the base of every lie, there is usually **fear** (God has not given us a spirit of fear), at the root of fear is usually **unbelief**—failure to trust in God through His provision of all that is ours in Christ, and not taking God at His Word. **Lies, fears, and unbelief---these are some of the strategies of the enemy!**

8. Look up these Scriptures and list the weapons that pull down (demolish) these strongly-held lies:
   - Hebrews 4:12-13

   - Revelation 12:11

   - Mark 16:17

 Spend some time thanking Him right now for His finished work on the cross for you!

Day Four

The Armor
Ephesians 6:14-17

Paul was in prison, most likely chained to a Roman soldier, when he wrote this letter to the Ephesian church. Paul would have been very familiar with the armor and what each piece meant to the soldier's protection and effectiveness.

1. What is the first piece of armor noted in verse 14? _____ Why do you think we are told to start with truth? To help you answer this, read John 14:6 and Romans 12:1-2. (What is another name for the enemy?)

2. What is the next piece of armor? Read the following related Scriptures and answer why you think this piece is so critical: Romans 1:17; 1 Corinthians 1:30; 2 Corinthians 5:21.

3. According to verse 15, what kind of shoes are we to wear? _____ See also Isaiah 52:7 and record your insights from this verse and also Ephesians 2:14 and Philippians 4:13. What do you see in these verses about using your mouth?

4. In verse 16, we are told to above all, take the shield of _____. According to 1 John 5:4-5, what overcomes? What do you think are the 'fiery darts' that Paul is talking about here? Where do 'darts' travel--by land or by air?! What was one of the names for the enemy in Ephesians 2:2?

5. According to Romans 10:17, how does faith come?

6. In verse 17 of Ephesians 6, what kind of helmet is it? Read Hebrews 5:9, Psalm 140:7, and Romans 12:1-2 and record further insights you receive regarding this piece of the armor.

7. The final piece of armor is the _____ of the _____, which is the _____ of _____. Whose sword does it belong to? _____ _____. Read Isaiah 55:11: What is the absolute truth about God's Word?

8. Read John 1:1, 4 and John 6:63: Record your insights from these verses regarding the Word of God.

Rhema-(hray-mah)-Strong's #4487-That which is said or spoken; an utterance in contrast to logos, which is the expression of a thought, a message, a discourse. Logos is the message; rhema is the communication of the message. Logos means the Bible in its entirety; rhema means a verse from the Bible. In Ephesians 6:17, this reference is to the particular verse that the believer takes (take the Sword of the Spirit) in the spiritual battle.

9. Our confidence in battle is not in our actions or even in the armor itself, according to Jude 24, our confidence is in _____!

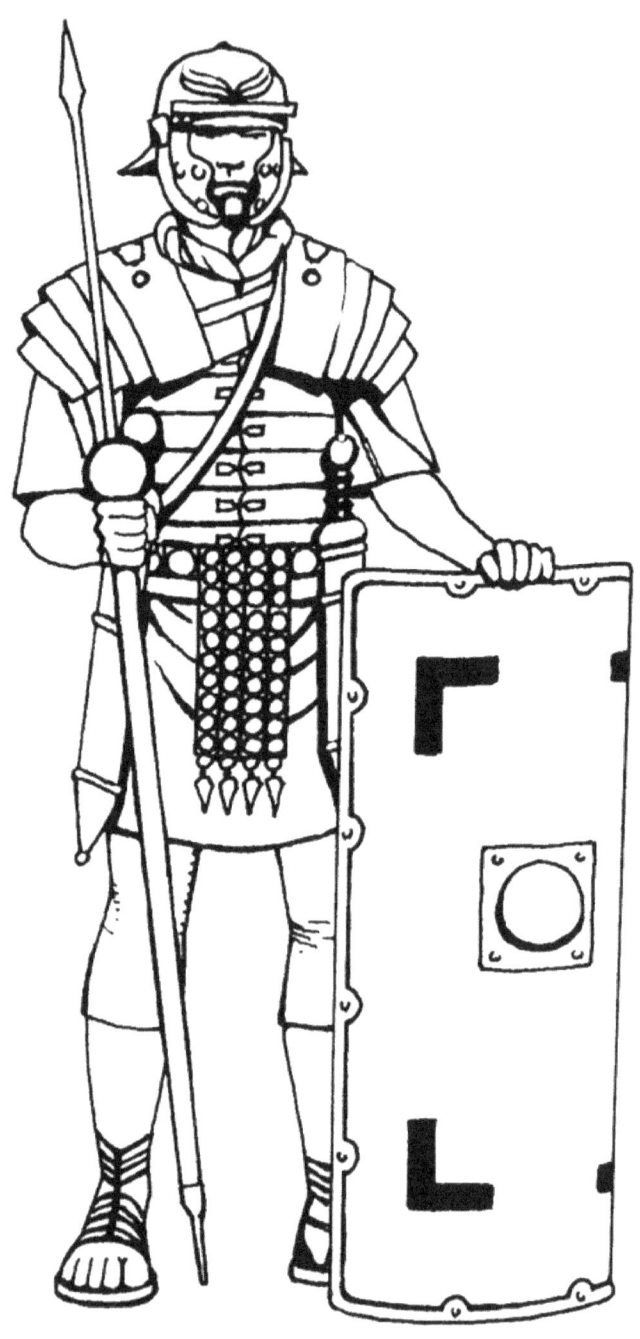

Day Five

Paul's Perfect Ending--Pray Always!
Ephesians 6:18-24

1. Read v. 18-20 and note Paul's final directive:

   Would you say this is part of the armor?

   What would you call this?

2. Look up the following verses and list the principles regarding "all prayer and supplication in the Spirit":

   - 1 John 5:14-15

   - John 14:13

   - John 15:7

   - James 5:16

   - James 1:6

   - John 14:14

   - Romans 8:26-27

- Jude 20

- 1 Corinthians 14:14-15

Our journey through Ephesians has been heavily based in Scriptural prayer. You've been instructed over and over again to formulate your own prayers based on the prayers of Paul and to pray them **aloud**. The above list of Scriptures is not at all exhaustive, but rather gives an outline of what could guide our prayer lives in an on-going way.

Prayer is the battle itself! God's Word is our chief weapon in all warfare and in all of life!

For your final prayer assignment, go back to yesterday's homework and the various pieces of armor. Write out your own prayer in the space below, 'dressing' yourself in the armor, 'clothed' with God's Word, ready to face the day.

3. In verse 19-20, Paul asks for prayer for himself. What is his prayer request and what do you think about it?

4. What is the ultimate focus or purpose of all spiritual warfare according to Colossians 4:3 and 1 Corinthians 16:9?

You are equipped! You've reached the end of our journey through the marvelous letter to the Ephesians! You, like Paul, are an ambassador—a representative of our Ruling Authority, JESUS CHRIST!!! Go and proclaim His Word boldly!

Special Equipping Section

Ephesians— The Majesty of Christ Revealed

Use this space to record how you see Jesus in each chapter as you study. The first few have been done for you.

From Ephesians 1:

v. 7--Redeemer

v. 10--The One in Whom and by Whom history will be consummated

v. 15--23-Resurrected Lord

      Reigning King

From Ephesians 2:

From Ephesians 3:

From Ephesians 4:

From Ephesians 5:

From Ephesians 6:

"Thanksgiving is our dialect."
(Ephesians 5:4 The Message)

Use this space to write down 3 things you are grateful for each day as you do the study. Giving thanks to God is your 'sacrifice of praise'.

Daily Declarations

Identity Markers Revealing Who I Am IN CHRIST

Your history is not your identity!

Your identity is based on the Word of God and what He says about you!

Do not put your faith or hope in this activity or method. Our faith is in Christ alone. Our daily declarations are merely an effective way to express our faith in God, based on His Word. We give 'voice' to the truth of God's Word!

"And they overcame him by the blood of the Lamb and by the word of their testimony…" Revelation 12:11 (NKJV)

Speaking God's Word Out Loud

Scripture Shows Us Why

"Death and life are in the power of the tongue, and those who love it will eat its fruit." (Proverbs 18:21 NKJV)

"Faith comes by hearing, and hearing by the Word of God." (Romans 10:17 NKJV)

"If you confess with your mouth the Lord Jesus and believe in your heart that God has raised Him from the dead, you will be saved. For with the heart one believes unto righteousness, and with the mouth confession is made unto salvation." (Romans 10: 9-10 NKJV)

"Therefore, holy brethren, partakers of the heavenly calling, consider the Apostle and High Priest of our confession, Christ Jesus." (Hebrews 3:1 NKJV)

"Seeing then that we have a great High Priest who has passed through the heavens, Jesus the Son of God, let us hold fast our confession." (Hebrews 4:14 NKJV)

"And since we have the same spirit of faith, according to what is written, 'I believed and therefore I spoke,' we also believe and therefore speak." (2 Corinthians 4:13 NKJV)

"For out of the abundance of the heart the mouth speaks. A good man out of the good treasure of his heart brings forth good things, and an evil man out of the evil treasure brings forth evil things. But I say to you that for every idle word men may speak, they will give account of it in the day of judgment. For by your words you will be justified, and by your words you will be condemned." (Matthew 12:34-37 NKJV)

"But what does it say? "The word is near you, in your mouth and in your heart" (that is, the word of faith which we preach).
(Romans 10:8 NKJV)

Bibliography

Unless otherwise noted, Scripture quotations are from *The New Spirit-Filled Life Bible.* Copyright 2002, Thomas Nelson, Inc., Publisher; and *The Holy Bible,* New King James Version. Copyright 1982, Thomas Nelson, Inc.

All Greek Word definitions noted are from *The New Spirit-Filled Life Bible.* Copyright 2002, Thomas Nelson, Inc., Publisher.

Scripture quotations noted Amplified are from *The Amplified Bible, Expanded Edition.* Copyright 1987, Zondervan Corporation and the Lockman Foundation.

Scripture quotations noted Message are from *The Message: The New Testament in Contemporary English,* Copyright 1993, Eugene H. Peterson. Pg.1611 Introduction to Ephesians.

Eldredge, John. *Epic-The Story God is Telling.* Nashville: Thomas Nelson Publishing, 2004.

Ortberg, Nancy. *Looking For God.* Tyndale House Publishers, 2008,

Thomas, Gary. *Sacred Parenting.* Grand Rapids: Zondervan, 2004.

About the Author:

Marjie Schaefer believes the Word of God is relevant, powerful, transformational, and life-giving to every single human being on the planet. She has spent her life investing in others and inviting them to join her in this pursuit of deeper truth.

As a result of her passion and pursuit, she has spent decades teaching women of all ages how to dig into the Word of God, and how to mine the treasures of it for themselves. She started in college and has continued on as a wife and mother, opening her heart and her home to those who hunger and thirst for more of God and His Word in their lives.

Marjie and her team currently lead the ministry, **Flourish Through the Word**, which is a community of women in the greater Seattle region committed to being equipped through God's Word. As a result of their time together in the Word, the women then move out into their arenas of influence, shining their lights for Jesus. You can find out more about this ministry, upcoming events and Bible studies, and the Flourish Conference at www.flourishthroughtheword.com. You can also sign up to receive regular email encouragements from Marjie.

Marjie has three previously published studies, _Grace Encounters_ and _Choose Joy_ and _Live Happy_.

Marjie has been married to Steve for 27 years and they have four children, a daughter Hayley, and sons Jordan, Matthew, and Luke.

www.ingramcontent.com/pod-product-compliance
Lightning Source LLC
Chambersburg PA
CBHW070550300426
44113CB00011B/1853